CHARLES KELLER

daffynitions

illustrated by
F. A. Fitzgerald

Prentice-Hall, Inc.,
Englewood Cliffs, N.J.

*For Barbara and Marilyn
and Ben and his men*

Book design by Cynthia Basil

Printed in the United States of America •J

Prentice-Hall International, Inc., London
Prentice-Hall of Australia, Pty. Ltd., North Sydney
Prentice-Hall of Canada, Ltd., Toronto
Prentice-Hall of India Private Ltd., New Delhi
Prentice-Hall of Japan, Inc., Tokyo

Library of Congress Cataloging in Publication Data

Keller, Charles.
    Daffynitions.

    SUMMARY: Text and cartoons offer humorous
definitions for a number of familiar words and
expressions.
    [1. Joke books] I. Fitzgerald, F. A. II. Title.
PZ8.7.K42Dof   818'.5'407   75-34280
ISBN 0-13-196584-0

announce
one-sixteenth of a pound

ant

a small hard-working insect that
always finds time to go to picnics

appear

something you fish off of

apricots
beds for monkeys

area code
a sinus condition

arrest

thing to take when you're tired

ash tray

a place where people put ashes
when the room doesn't have a rug

acorn
an oak in a nutshell

afford
a car some people drive

attack
a small nail

auctioneer
a man who looks forbidding

autograph
a chart showing sale of cars

axe
chopstick

bacteria
the rear of a cafeteria

barber shop
a clip joint

bathing beauty
a girl worth wading for

bee
a hum-bug

beet

a potato with high blood pressure

buccaneer

too much to pay for corn

chicken farm
a large egg plant

commentator
an ordinary spud

conceit
I-strain

crowbar
a bird's drinking place

camelot
a parking lot for camels

carbuncle
an auto collision

cartoon
a song you hear on the car radio

chair
headquarters for hindquarters

denial
where Cleopatra lived

dentist

someone who always looks
down in the mouth

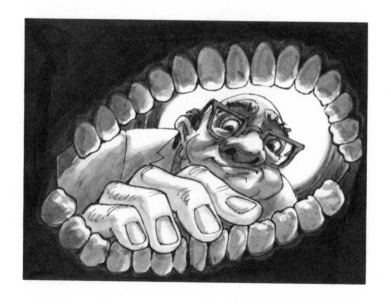

diploma
the man who fixes the pipes

drill sergeant

an Army dentist

egg
a fowl ball

English Channel
a British T.V. station

eraser
what the artist's wife said when
he drew a beautiful girl

extinct

a dead skunk

gallows
where no noose is good noose

goblet

a small turkey

gossip
letting the chat out of the bag

hamburger

steak that didn't pass its physical

hay

grass a-la-mode

hogwash
pig's laundry

home run

a thing you do in a ball game
when the ball goes through a
window

ice
skid stuff

igloo
an icicle built for two

illegal

a sick bird

incongruous

where the laws are made

indistinct

where you put the dirty dishes

information
how Air Force planes fly

jaywalking

an exercise that brings that run-down feeling

jump
the last word in an airplane

kidney

knee of a baby goat

kindred

a fear of relatives coming

knob
a thing to adore

leopard

a dotted lion

license number
the best thing to take when
you're run down

melancholy
a dog that likes watermelons

mistletoe

astronaut's athlete's foot

motel
William Tell's brother

mummy

an Egyptian pressed for time

mushroom

the place where they make the
school lunch

nail

a long, round object with a flat
head which you aim at while you
hit your thumb

nursery
a bawl park

operetta

a girl who works for the phone
company

ottoman

a car mechanic

out-of-bounds
a tired kangeroo

paradox
two doctors

paratrooper
an Army dropout

pea

a vegeta-pill

pigeon-toed
half-pigeon, half toad

propaganda

a socially correct goose

panhandler
dishwasher

parole
a cell-out

pickle
a cucumber in a sour mood

pillow
headquarters

pink elephant
a beast of bourbon

pretzel
a double-jointed doughnut

printer
a man of letters

quadruplets
four crying out loud

racetrack

the only place where windows
clean people

raisin
a worried grape

rebate

putting another worm on the hook

romance
ants in Rome

rhubarb
bloodshot celery

ringleader
first one in the bath tub

rug
something that is sold by the yard
and worn by the feet

shotgun
a worn-out gun

sleeping bag
a nap sack

snoring
sheet music

southpaw
a daddy from Dixie

square root
diced carrots

tears
glum drops

tongue twister
when you get your tang tongueled

Trojan horse
phony pony

unabridged

a river you have to swim to cross

undercover agent

spy in bed

vitamin

what you do when someone
comes to the house

volcano

a mountain with a built-in
barbeque pit

walkie-talkie
a grounded parrot.

washable
to bathe a bull

water cooler
thirst aid kit

wind
air in a hurry

woe
opposite of giddy-up

x-ray
bellyvision

yellow
what you do when you stub your
toe

zebra

a horse that escaped from prison

zookeeper
a critter-sitter.